STARTING POINT
SCIENCE

Susan Mayes

Designed by Mike Pringle
Series editor: Heather Amery

CONTENTS

WHAT MAKES IT RAIN?

Illustrated by Richard Deverell and Mike Pringle

CONTENTS

Susan Mayes

All about rain

When gray clouds start to fill the sky, this often means that rain is on the way.

The rainwater runs down drains, or into streams, rivers and lakes. Some of it makes puddles on the ground.

Sometimes there is too much rain and sometimes there is not enough. When the air is cold snow may fall.

When the rain stops and the sun comes out, puddles on the ground get smaller and smaller.

Where does the water go when it dries up? How does water get into the sky to make more rain?

What is a weather forecast and how is it made? You can find out about these things in this part of the book.

3

Where the water goes

After a shower of rain, heat from the sun begins to dry up all the water on the ground.

The water turns into tiny droplets in the air, leaving the ground dry. The droplets are so small that you cannot see them. They are called water vapor.

When water dries up, this is called evaporation.

Try this

On a hot day, try this experiment to make water dry up.

Put two plates in a sunny place with a spoonful of water in each one.

Shade one plate with a book.

Look at the plates every hour.

The water in the sun dries up first. Water always evaporates more quickly in the hot sun than it does in the cool shade.

Heating up

If a pan without a lid boils on a high heat for a long time, the water will evaporate and the food burns.

4

Warm air

When air is warmed, it rises. You cannot see it moving, but you can sometimes see how it takes things up, high into the sky.

Smoke from a fire rises up the chimney and into the sky.

Warm air from a bonfire carries sparks and bits of ash upwards.

Try this

Hold a very thin piece of tissue paper over a heater.

The air warmed by the heater rises and lifts the paper.

The sun's heat

Warm air and water vapor.

Air rises when it is warmed by the sun. It carries water vapor from the land and sea up into the sky.

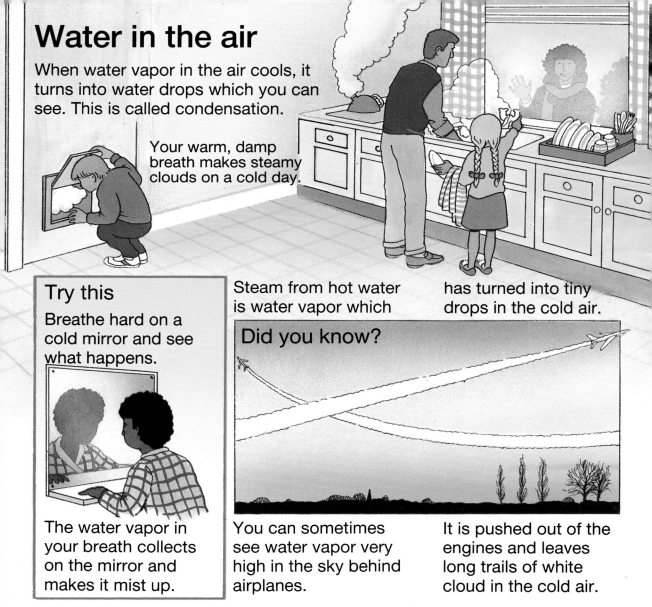

Water in the air

When water vapor in the air cools, it turns into water drops which you can see. This is called condensation.

Your warm, damp breath makes steamy clouds on a cold day.

Steam from hot water is water vapor which has turned into tiny drops in the cold air.

Try this

Breathe hard on a cold mirror and see what happens.

The water vapor in your breath collects on the mirror and makes it mist up.

Did you know?

You can sometimes see water vapor very high in the sky behind airplanes.

It is pushed out of the engines and leaves long trails of white cloud in the cold air.

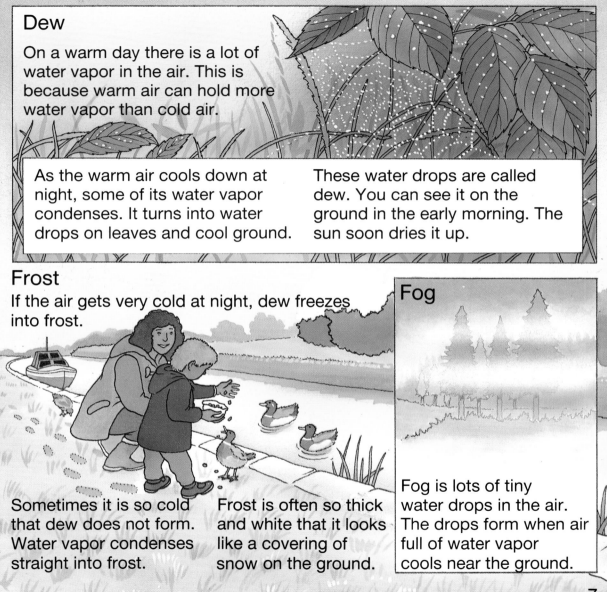

Dew

On a warm day there is a lot of water vapor in the air. This is because warm air can hold more water vapor than cold air.

As the warm air cools down at night, some of its water vapor condenses. It turns into water drops on leaves and cool ground.

These water drops are called dew. You can see it on the ground in the early morning. The sun soon dries it up.

Frost

If the air gets very cold at night, dew freezes into frost.

Sometimes it is so cold that dew does not form. Water vapor condenses straight into frost.

Frost is often so thick and white that it looks like a covering of snow on the ground.

Fog

Fog is lots of tiny water drops in the air. The drops form when air full of water vapor cools near the ground.

7

Cold air

The heat from the sun bounces off the ground and warms the air near it. The air higher up in the sky is much colder. It is so cold that high mountain tops are snowy all year.

How clouds form

Every day water from the sea evaporates in the sun.

The warm air near the ground carries the water vapor up into the sky.

The cold air makes the water vapor condense into groups of tiny drops or ice crystals. We see them as clouds.

Did you know?

In some parts of the world people can sunbathe on a beach and see snow on the high mountains.

8

Above the clouds

When you take off in an airplane, you can go through the clouds and fly above them. The sun shines up there all the time during the day.

Inside a cloud

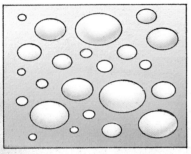  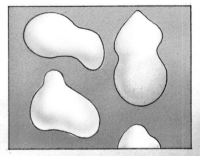

The millions of tiny water droplets which make a rain cloud are different sizes.

Big drops fall and bump into smaller ones. They join and make bigger drops.

When the water drops are heavy enough they fall to Earth as drops of rain.

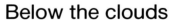

Below the clouds

The rainwater collects in seas, lakes, rivers and puddles. When it stops raining the sun will start to dry up this water.

Snowy weather

How snowflakes form

Most water drops in high clouds freeze into tiny specks of ice in the cold air.

As they fall, more water freezes on them. They become ice crystals.

When the crystals are big enough, they join together and fall as snowflakes.

Falling snowflakes soften in warmer air. They stick together easily. Sticky snow makes good snowballs.

Snowflake facts

All snowflakes are a six-sided shape.

Millions of snowflakes have fallen to Earth, but nobody has ever found two which are exactly the same.

Did you know?

People have seen huge snowflakes the size of large plates.

Avalanches

A skier or a loud noise can start an avalanche.

An avalanche is lots of snow which slides down a steep mountain slope. This may happen when the weather gets warmer and snow starts to melt.

Hail

Hailstones are hard lumps of ice which form inside a storm cloud. They fall to the ground very quickly in a hailstorm.

Raindrops freeze into ice pellets at the top of a storm cloud.

Air currents toss them up and down. More water freezes on to them.

When the pellets are too heavy to stay up, they fall as hailstones.

Inside a hailstone

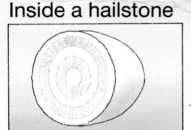

If you cut a hailstone you would see the layers of frozen water.

Did you know?

The biggest hailstone ever was 19cm (7½in) across, which is nearly as big as a football.

Hailstone damage

Big hailstones can make dents in cars and break windows. A bad hailstorm can flatten a field of corn in just a few minutes.

11

Rainbows

Next time it rains and the sun is shining at the same time, look for a rainbow.

How a rainbow is made

A ray of light looks white but it is really made up of many colors.

When sun shines through a raindrop the water splits the light into all its colors.

sunlight

← *raindrop*

The colors bounce off the back of the drop and bend as they come out.

A rainbow appears when sunlight shines on falling drops of water in a waterfall.

Rainbow colors

There are seven main colors in a rainbow and they are always in the same order – red, orange, yellow, green, blue, indigo and violet.

Try this

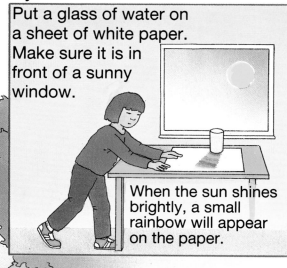

Put a glass of water on a sheet of white paper. Make sure it is in front of a sunny window.

When the sun shines brightly, a small rainbow will appear on the paper.

Thunderstorms

Tall, dark clouds often bring a storm with thunder and flashes of lightning.

What is lightning?

A kind of electricity, called static electricity, starts to build up in a storm cloud.

When there is too much, it jumps from the cloud in a huge, hot spark. This spark is the flash of lightning which you see in the sky.

Why we hear thunder

A flash of lightning heats the air around it very quickly. It starts a huge wave of air which grows bigger and bigger. This makes the thunder which you hear.

Lightning can go from cloud to cloud, or from the cloud down to the ground.

Try this

Make your own spark of static electricity.

Press a large lump of clay onto a tin tray to make a handle.

Hold the clay and rub the tray round and round on top of a thick plastic bag.

In the dark hold something metal near the corner of the tray. Watch the spark jump away.

Water on the ground

In a town, rainwater runs down the drains. It is carried away by underground pipes.

In the country, rainwater runs down slopes and into streams, rivers and lakes. Some soaks into the ground.

As a stream flows along, it is joined by more water from springs and from under the ground.

A river finds the easiest way across the land.

The water trickles down through the soil. It goes into underground streams and wells, then it travels on under the ground.

Sometimes underground water comes out of the side of a hill as a spring. Most streams start from a spring in this way.

Snow and ice melt when the weather warms up. The water runs away and soaks into the ground.

As the rivers, streams and springs make their way to the sea, some of their water evaporates.

More streams join together and they form a river.

A small river which flows into a bigger one is called a tributary.

Some water collects in hollows in the ground. This is how lakes are formed.

The river mouth is where the water runs out into the sea and ends its journey.

Water evaporates from the sea every day. The tiny invisible droplets will soon collect to make more clouds.

15

Too much rain

A flood sometimes happens when there is a very heavy rainstorm, or if it rains for a long time. The water cannot all seep away into the ground and it runs on to the land. Streams and rivers overflow with water.

Snow and ice

Floods sometimes happen in the spring when snow and ice start to melt. The water cannot soak into the soil because the ground is still frozen hard underneath.

Stopping the water

A dam is a wall which is built across a river to make a lake. It holds the water back and can also be used to control floods.

A sudden flood

A flood which happens very suddenly is called a flash flood. It happens when a huge amount of rain falls in one place in a very short time.

There was a flash flood in New South Wales, Australia, in April 1989. The water swept away roads, bridges, cars, buildings and animals.

Living with rain

People in Indonesia build houses on stilts. They will be safe above the water when the floods come.

Moving away

The people of Barotseland, Zambia, move away when the floodwaters come. They take all their belongings to higher ground.

The driest places

Drought

In some places it does not rain for many weeks. There is not enough water to drink or grow plants. This dry time is called a drought.

Did you know?

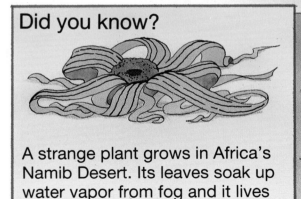

A strange plant grows in Africa's Namib Desert. Its leaves soak up water vapor from fog and it lives for at least a thousand years.

Deserts are the driest places in the world. In some places it does not rain for years. Any water evaporates quickly in the hot sunshine.

Cacti are desert plants which store the water they need in their stems.

In the United States, water from the Colorado river runs along canals to the Sonoran Desert. It is pumped onto the dry land to grow crops.

The long roots of the mesquite plant find water 53m (174ft) under the ground.

Kangaroo rats never drink. Their bodies have a special way of making water from the dry seeds which they eat.

Did you know?

A camel can live for as long as ten days in the desert without drinking.

Its body slowly turns fat in the hump into the water it needs.

Desert flowers

Seeds of flowers lie in the dry soil waiting for rain. When it falls, the flowers bloom very quickly but they only live for a day or two.

What kind of weather?

A weather forecast tells you what the weather is going to be like. You can see it on television, hear it on the radio or read it in the newspaper.

Weather forecasts can help you decide what to wear or where to go for the day.

People who need to know

An aircraft pilot needs to know what the weather will be like on the flight.

A fisherman needs to know if the weather at sea is going to be fine or stormy.

A farmer uses weather forecasts every day. He needs good weather for a lot of his work.

Making a weather forecast

A weather station is where facts about the weather are collected at certain times every day.

More facts come from satellites which study the weather from space.

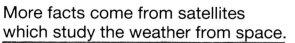

They measure the wind speed and the water vapor in the air. They even measure the temperature.

Forecasters collect facts from weather stations around the world and from satellites. They use the facts to make weather charts.

They use these charts to help make a weather forecast. This tells you what the weather will be like over the next few days.

21

Useful words

You can find these words in this part of the book. The pictures will help you remember what the words mean.

canal
This is a special waterway built for ships and to carry water across land.

condensation
This is tiny drops of water you see on cold things. It forms when warm, damp air touches something cold.

dam
This is a wall built to hold water back and make a lake.

desert
This is a dry place, where it hardly ever rains. Only a few plants grow.

dew
This is the name for the small drops of water which form on cool ground, leaves and plants.

evaporate
This is what happens when water dries up. It turns into tiny, invisible water drops in the air.

flood

This is when lots of water covers the land, after too much rain.

frost

This is tiny drops of frozen water which appear on the ground and on other things in cold weather.

hail

This is the name for lumps of ice which form in a storm cloud.

fog

This is tiny drops of water which you can see in the air. It looks like patches of low cloud.

water vapor

This is the name for tiny droplets of water in the air. The droplets are so small you cannot see them.

weather satellite

This is a machine sent into space to study the weather around the Earth.

23

Making a weather chart

Trace this chart on to a piece of paper. Go outside every morning and afternoon to see what the weather is like, then choose the right weather sign to put in the box. There may be two kinds of weather.

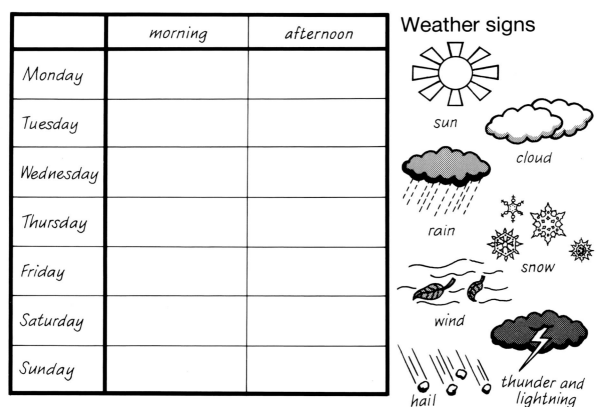

	morning	afternoon
Monday		
Tuesday		
Wednesday		
Thursday		
Friday		
Saturday		
Sunday		

Weather signs

sun

cloud

rain

snow

wind

hail

thunder and lightning

Does the weather change much? Has it been sunny or cloudy? Has there been rain or snow?

You could make up some new weather signs yourself. Can you think of one for frost or fog?

WHAT MAKES A FLOWER GROW?

Illustrated by Brin Edwards and Mike Pringle

Susan Mayes

CONTENTS

All about flowers

Thousands of different flowers grow all over the world. They grow in gardens, on vegetables, on trees, in streets, in hedges and in your home.

Flowers are all kinds of colors, shapes and sizes. Some of them have very strong smells.

Insects and other tiny animals visit them. Most flowers die each year and grow again later.

26

Some flowers live in very hot countries and others live in cold places. Very strange flowers grow in some parts of the world.

Why do flowers have different colors and smells? Why do they grow again and what do they need to grow well?

What are the strangest flowers? You can find out about all of these things in this part of the book.

Taking a close look

If you look closely at a flower, you can see that it has different parts. Each part has a special job.

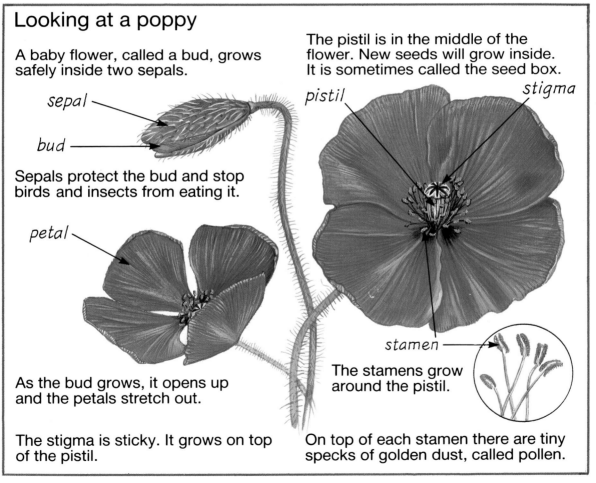

Looking at a poppy

A baby flower, called a bud, grows safely inside two sepals.

sepal

bud

Sepals protect the bud and stop birds and insects from eating it.

petal

As the bud grows, it opens up and the petals stretch out.

The stigma is sticky. It grows on top of the pistil.

The pistil is in the middle of the flower. New seeds will grow inside. It is sometimes called the seed box.

pistil

stigma

stamen

The stamens grow around the pistil.

On top of each stamen there are tiny specks of golden dust, called pollen.

Different flowers

Most flowers have the same main parts, but they are all kinds of different colors, shapes and sizes.

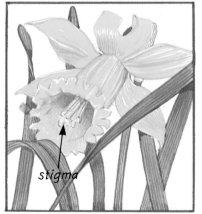

A yellow water lily has big sepals around the outside and lots of short petals in the middle.

sepal

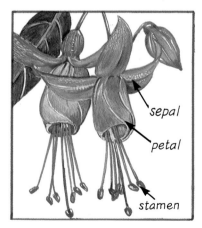

sepal

petal

stamen

Fuchsias have long stamens and colorful sepals and petals.

stigma

A daffodil has one long stigma which grows from the pistil.

The petals of the snapdragon are all joined together.

Who visits a flower?

Flowers all over the world are visited by small animals, birds and many kinds of insects.

Most animals go to flowers to look for pollen and sweet liquid food inside, called nectar.

Honey bees visit all kinds of flowers, looking for food to store for the winter.

Tiny birds

A hummingbird hovers in front of brightly colored flowers to drink the nectar with its long beak.

Bats

In some countries, bats fly to flowers which open in the evening. They search for nectar and pollen.

Butterflies settle on buddleia flowers to drink nectar with their long tongues.

A bumble bee crawls into a foxglove to find the sweet food.

Flower signals

Many flowers use special signals which make the insects and tiny creatures come to visit them.

Colors

Special colors and markings guide bees to flowers and show them where to find the pollen inside.

You cannot see some markings but bees can. They do not see colors and shapes the same way as we do.

Smells

Most flowers have a sweet smell. It comes from the petals and tells visitors there is food nearby.

Honeysuckle has a strong smell at night. This is when the moths come out to find nectar for food.

A nasty smell

Flies visit a stapelia flower to lay their eggs. They come because it looks and smells like rotting meat.

Visitors at work

Insects and other small animals help plants when visiting them for food.

They carry pollen from flower to flower. This will make seeds grow.

When a bee lands on a flower, some pollen from the stamens rubs off on to its body.

The bee flies to the next flower and some pollen rubs off on to the flower's stigma.

More pollen sticks to the bee as it crawls around on each flower it visits.

Open or closed

Flowers are not open to visitors if the weather is bad. They close to keep the pollen dry and safe.

A day-time flower closes up its petals at night to stop the dew from wetting the pollen inside.

Pollen in the air

Some plants do not need visitors. They do not have special colors or smells because their pollen is carried from plant to plant by the wind.

Tiny grains

Some trees have flowers called catkins. Their tiny, golden grains of pollen blow away in the wind.

Grass has flowers at the top of the stalk. The pollen is high up so it blows away easily.

Pollen clouds

In the summer, you sometimes see clouds of pollen in the air. People with hay fever sneeze and sneeze.

Did you know?

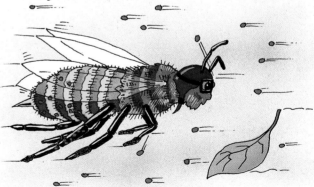

Pollen grains carried by flower visitors are sticky, but pollen grains in the air are smooth and dry.

33

All about seeds

A plant cannot grow seeds until pollen reaches its stigma. And the pollen must be from the same kind of plant.

pollen

stigma

stigma

eggs

seed box

Grains of pollen, carried by visitors, or blown by the wind, land on a new flower. They stick to the stigma.

The grains travel down into the tiny eggs inside the seed box. They make the eggs grow into seeds.

stamen

The flower does not need the petals and stamens any more, so they drop off. Only the seed box is left.

The seeds grow inside until they are ripe. The seeds of this plant leave through small holes.

Kinds of seeds

Many different plants have seeds which you can eat.

Sweet chestnuts, walnuts and coconuts are three kinds of seeds which come from trees.

Sunflower seeds are used to make oil and margarine. You can also eat them from the flower.

Inside and outside

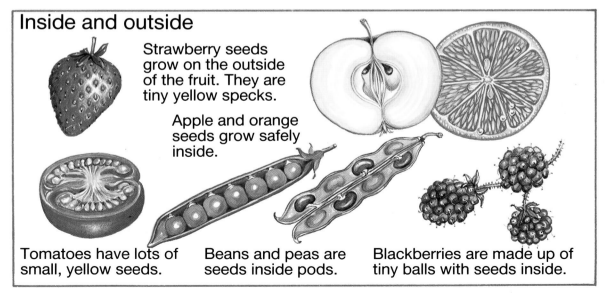

Strawberry seeds grow on the outside of the fruit. They are tiny yellow specks.

Apple and orange seeds grow safely inside.

Tomatoes have lots of small, yellow seeds.

Beans and peas are seeds inside pods.

Blackberries are made up of tiny balls with seeds inside.

Seeds on the move

Popping out

The seeds of an iris grow inside colorful, round fruit. When the fruit is ripe, the seeds leave by popping out on to the ground.

Old Man's Beard

This is the name for the big, fluffy balls from a clematis plant. They are carried by the wind, with the seeds inside.

Seeds leave plants in different ways. Most of them are blown in the wind or are carried by animals.

Birds like to eat brightly colored seeds. They carry them away.

Seeds with hooks or sticky hairs, stick to birds and animals.

Conkers are the seeds of horse chestnut trees. They fall to the ground in green, spiky cases.

Seeds from a sycamore tree spin to the ground like helicopters.

Dandelion seeds blow away in the wind.

When poppy seeds are ripe, they pop out of the pod.

Ants carry some seeds away and store them for winter food.

Many of the seeds will die or be eaten but some are covered by soil or leaves. They stay there all winter until spring comes.

Rolling along

Tumbleweeds grow in America. When their seeds are ripe the plant curls into a ball. It rolls along in the wind, scattering the seeds.

The fastest seeds

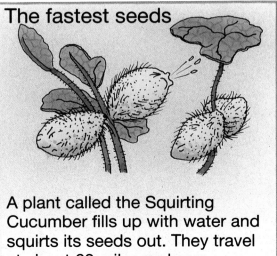

A plant called the Squirting Cucumber fills up with water and squirts its seeds out. They travel at about 60 miles an hour.

Roots and shoots

In the spring, days grow longer and warmer. Seeds get the warmth and rain they need to make them grow.

Leaves and sunlight

The seeds split and shoots grow up towards the light.

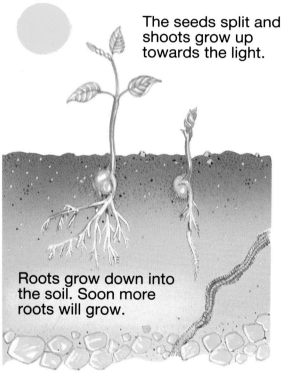

Little seed leaves feed the plant until the big leaves grow. Leaves have a special way of using air and sunlight to make plant food.

Roots grow down into the soil. Soon more roots will grow.

Growing beans

Put some paper towels in a jar with some water.

Put some beans next to the glass.

The roots feed the plant with water and goodness from the soil. They also hold the plant in the ground.

Put the jar in a warm, light place. The beans will swell up until they split and sprout roots and shoots.

Waterways

Plants suck up the water they need through their waterways. These are very thin tubes inside the stems.

Try this

You will need:

a big jar
some food dye
some white flowers

In the soil

Worms pull leaves down into the soil.

Soil is full of things which are good for plants. Dead leaves, plants and tiny creatures rot away and make good plant food.

Put some water in the jar and add a few drops of food dye. Stand the flowers in it. After a few days the petal tips will change color.

In two more days, the flowers will be the same color as the dye. This is because the flowers suck the water and dye up into the petals.

Things you can grow

You can buy packets of flower and vegetable seeds in the shops. Here are some of the things you will need when you plant seeds for yourself.

plant pots or yogurt pots
a bag of compost
a small watering can or jug
a little trowel or an old spoon
a plate and some kitchen towels
cress and sunflower seeds

Compost is a special soil with rich plant food in it.

Growing cress

Cress grows very easily and quickly at any time of the year.

Your cress will be ready to eat when it is about 3 ins high.

You do not need soil, just some damp kitchen towels on a plate. Sprinkle some cress seeds on top.

Put the plate in a light place. The tiny shoots will soon grow, but you must keep the towels damp.

Sunflowers

In the spring you can start to grow sunflower seeds in pots.

Use a pot of compost for each seed. Push the seed in and sprinkle a little compost on top. Water the pots and put them in a warm, sunny place.

Try measuring the sunflowers to see how tall they grow.

After a few weeks shoots will appear and the plants will grow bigger. When they have four leaves they are big enough to plant in the garden.

Remember

Plants need these things to help them grow well.

They need sunlight to help them make their own special plant food.

They need water, but not too much, or they may rot.

They need soil because it gives them water and food.

Where flowers grow

In the town

Gardens and parks are not the only places in towns where you might find flowers growing.

Some seeds are blown on to the roofs, where they grow.

Dandelion seeds get into the cracks in pavements.

The sowthistle grows in waste places and by the roadside.

Ivy-leaved toadflax grows on walls. It has purple flowers.

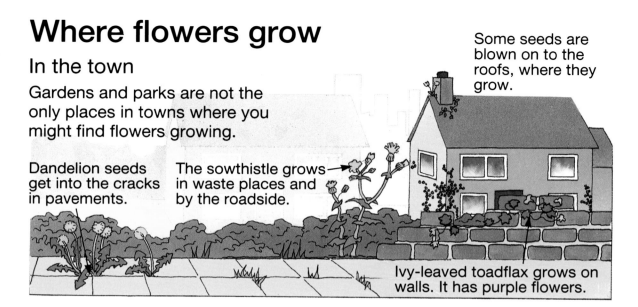

In the country

Many wild flowers grow in different countries all over the world. These flowers grow in Europe.

The sweet briar has pink flowers and prickly stems.

The red horse chestnut tree has groups of flowers.

The white dead-nettle has white flowers.

The flowers of the wild cherry tree smell very sweet.

In hot places

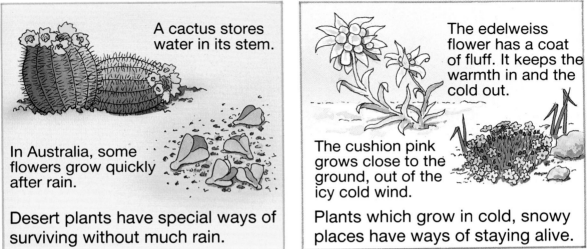

A cactus stores water in its stem.

In Australia, some flowers grow quickly after rain.

Desert plants have special ways of surviving without much rain.

In cold places

The edelweiss flower has a coat of fluff. It keeps the warmth in and the cold out.

The cushion pink grows close to the ground, out of the icy cold wind.

Plants which grow in cold, snowy places have ways of staying alive.

By the water

Some flowers grow well by the sea, by streams and other damp places.

Sea holly grows on beaches. It has spiky leaves and light blue flowers.

The marsh marigold likes ditches and wet places.

Sea bindweed has pink flowers with white stripes. It likes sandy beaches.

Water crowfoot floats on top of the water.

43

Amazing plant facts

Many strange plants and flowers grow in parts of the world. They are all sorts of amazing shapes and sizes. Some even eat small animals.

The biggest flowers

The rafflesia flower is also very smelly.

The flower of the rafflesia plant is the biggest flower in the world. It measures nearly a yard across.

The giant cactus

The saguaro is the largest cactus in the world. It grows as high as 50 feet and lives for over 200 years.

Tiny plants

The smallest flowering plant is a kind of duckweed. It is so tiny that it looks like scum on the water.

Flower traps

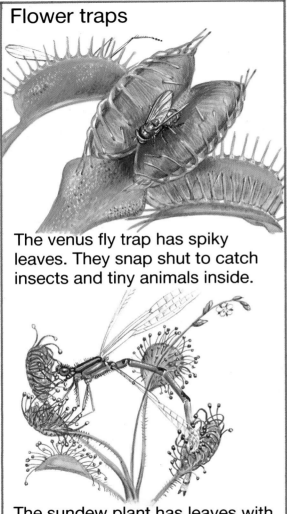

The venus fly trap has spiky leaves. They snap shut to catch insects and tiny animals inside.

The sundew plant has leaves with sticky blobs. Insects stick to them and are eaten as plant food.

The oldest potted plant

A man grew a plant in a pot in Vienna in 1801. It is still alive and will soon be 200 years old.

The strongest water lily

The victoria amazonica water lily is strong enough for a child to stand on its thick, floating leaves.

Useful words

You can find these words in this part of the book. The pictures will help you remember what the words mean.

hay fever
People with hay fever sneeze when there is a lot of pollen in the air.

insect
This is a small animal with 6 legs and a body made of 3 parts. A bee is an insect.

nectar
This is sweet liquid food inside a flower. Small visitors come to drink it. Bees use it to make honey.

pistil
New seeds grow in this part of the flower. It is also called the seed box.

pollen
This is the name for tiny golden specks on a flower. It makes new seeds grow in another flower.

roots
These parts of a plant grow down into the ground. They take in water and goodness from the soil.

sepals

These wrap around a bud to keep it safe while it is growing.

shoots

These are the new parts of a plant.

stamen

This part of a flower has pollen at the end.

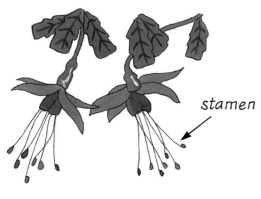

stamen

stem

This is the stalk of a plant. It holds the flowers up, above the ground.

stigma

This flower part is sticky. Pollen from another flower sticks to it easily.

stigma

waterways

These are thin tubes inside a plant stem. The plant drinks water through them, to stay alive and to grow.

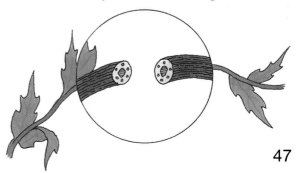

Flower puzzle

Here are 10 different kinds of flowers. They are all in this part of the book.

Can you find them and learn their names? The answers are at the bottom of this page.

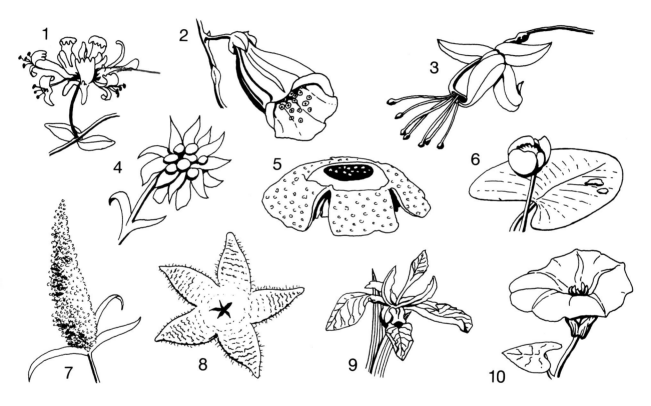

Answers

1. honeysuckle 2. foxglove 3. fuchsia 4. edelweiss 5. rafflesia 6. yellow water lily 7. buddleia 8. stapelia 9. iris 10. sea bindweed

WHERE DOES ELECTRICITY COME FROM?

Illustrated by John Shackell and John Scorey

Susan Mayes

CONTENTS

Electricity at work

Electricity gives power, light and heat to cities, towns and villages all over the world.

Electricity makes street lights work and powers a high speed train.

It can travel long distances to work in places far away.

You cannot see electricity but you can see where it is working around you, all the time.

How is electricity made? How does it get to your home and what can it do?

You can find out about all of these things in this part of the book.

Electricity and light

The first electric light bulb was made by Thomas Edison over 100 years ago, in 1879. Now millions of them are used all over the world.

How many light bulbs can you count in and around your home?

Inside a light bulb

When you turn on a switch, electricity goes through the wires into the bulb.

It goes into a thin coil of wire, called a filament, and makes it heat up.

Did you know?

Some lighthouses use lamps which are 20 times brighter than bulbs in your home.

filament

The filament is made of a metal called tungsten, which gets hot without melting.

It gets hotter and hotter until it glows white. This glow is the light you see.

Special mirrors make the light shine as far as 24 miles out across the sea.

Electricity can be very dangerous. Never play with it.

Electricity and heat

Special wires which carry electricity heat up when the electricity flows through them.

Hot wires are very useful because they heat up all sorts of things.

An electric heater has heating wires inside. When electricity goes through them, they get hot and the heater warms the room.

Electricity heats coils of wire in a hairdryer. A fan blows air over the hot wires. This heats up the air so you can dry your hair.

On most electric ranges, each ring has a heating wire inside. The electricity flows through and heats the ring, so you can cook on it.

Did you know?

Some soccer fields have heating wires under the ground.

They stop the field from freezing when the weather is cold.

Never use anything electrical near water.

How a battery works

Some toys need a small amount of electricity to make them work. They get it from a battery.

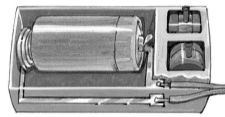

Inside the battery, special chemicals work together to make the electricity. It then travels through the wires to make the toy work. The battery stops working when the chemicals are used up.

Things which use batteries

A digital watch uses electricity from a tiny, thin battery.

A flashlight bulb lights up when electricity from the batteries passes through it.

A car has a special, powerful battery. Its electricity makes the engine, lights and heater work.

Try this

Ask a grown-up to help you try this.
To light up a bulb you will need:
2 pieces of flex – wire covered with plastic
a 1.5 volt flashlight battery, a 1.5 volt
    flashlight bulb and a bulb holder
sticky tape and a small screwdriver
a pair of scissors

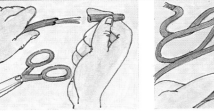

Screw the bulb into the bulb holder.	Strip off the plastic at each end of the wire.	Fix the end of one wire to the bulb holder.

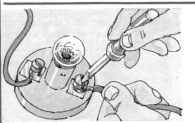

Fix the second piece of wire to the other side of the holder.	Use sticky tape to fix one piece of wire to each end of the battery.	Watch the bulb light up when the electricity passes through it.

Electricity which moves along a wire is called electric current.

If the current cannot go along its path, or circuit, the light goes off.

How a telephone works

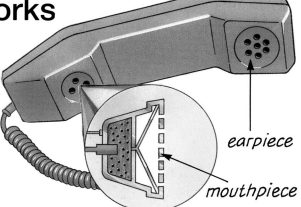

earpiece

mouthpiece

When you dial a number, an electric message goes to the telephone exchange. It tells the machine in the exchange which telephone to ring.

There is a microphone inside the mouthpiece. It changes the sound of your voice into electric signals which can be sent along cables.

Some cables go under the sea to take messages to other countries.

The person you are talking to hears you through the earpiece.

Some cables go overground but most go underground. The signals can travel thousands of miles.

There is a tiny loudspeaker inside the earpiece. It changes the signals back into the sound of your voice.

About television

Electricity makes your television work as soon as you switch on.

It brings you the pictures you see and the sounds you hear.

How it works

A television camera turns pictures into electric signals.

The signals travel along a cable to a television transmitter.

The television antenna on your house picks up the signals.

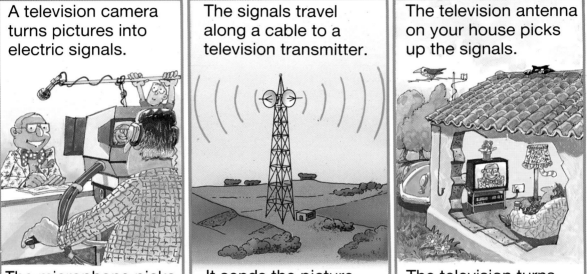

The microphone picks up sounds and turns them into more signals.

It sends the picture and sound signals through the air.

The television turns the signals back into pictures and sounds.

Did you know?

In space, machines called satellites can pick up electrical signals from radios, telephones and televisions. They send them round the world.

The signals are sent by a big transmitter.

Electricity to your home

Electricity is made in a power station. At the power station it is fed into a transformer.

The transformer makes the electricity stronger so lots of power can be sent to people who need it.

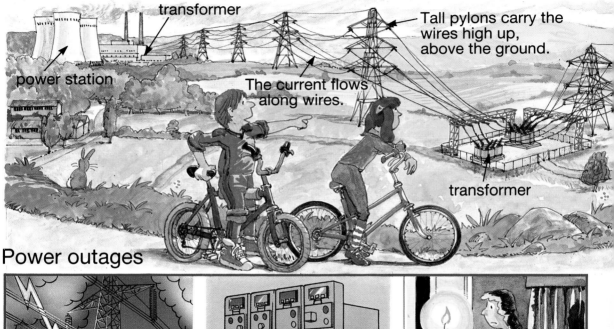

transformer

Tall pylons carry the wires high up, above the ground.

power station

The current flows along wires.

transformer

Power outages

Sometimes, lightning strikes a power line and damages it.

Circuit breakers stop electricity flowing along the broken part.

Some people have no electricity until the line is mended.

Electricity is fed around the country to other transformers. They make it weaker, so you can use it at home.

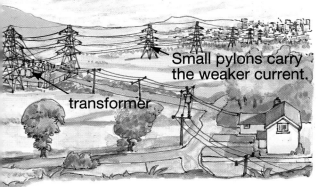

Small pylons carry the weaker current.

transformer

Under the ground
In some towns, electric cables go under the ground. They bring the current into your home.

Workmen often dig up the road to repair the cables underneath.

In the house

The wires which carry power round your house are hidden safely in walls, in ceilings or under floors.

Plugging in
Electricity makes tools, lamps and electrical machines work anywhere you can plug them in.

The plug fits into a socket at the wall. When it is switched on, the electricity goes along the wire.

How electricity is made

The electricity which is used in your home is made in different kinds of power stations.

Using coal and oil

Coal and oil were made millions of years ago, deep inside the Earth. They are used in some power stations to make electricity.

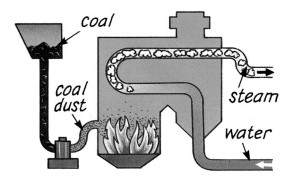

The coal and oil is burned in a boiler to heat water. When the water gets very hot, it turns into steam.

The steam goes along pipes to a machine called a turbine. It pushes against the metal blades and makes them spin very fast.

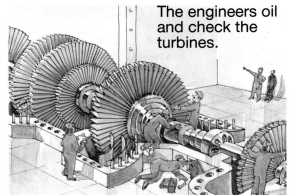

The engineers oil and check the turbines.

As the turbine spins, it works a machine called a generator. This makes the electricity.

Nuclear power stations

Nuclear power stations use fuel called uranium. It is dug out of the ground and used in a special way to make electricity.

The reactor

The uranium is made into rods. Inside the power station, they are put into the reactor. They are used to make heat.

Visitors can stand behind a window to look at the refuelling machine.

Uranium sends out something dangerous which you cannot see, called radiation. A concrete shield round the reactor keeps it safe.

Water and steam

The heat made in the reactor boils water in pipes. This turns into steam which goes to the turbines.

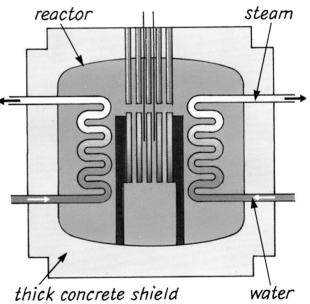

reactor

steam

thick concrete shield

water

The steam spins the turbines. They work the generator, which makes electricity like generators in other power stations.

Power from water

A hydro-electric power station uses falling water to make electricity. The water comes from a huge lake called a reservoir.

The turbines

At the bottom of each pipeline the water works the turbine runner.

turbine runner

blade

water

It pushes against the metal blades to make the runner turn quickly.

The generator

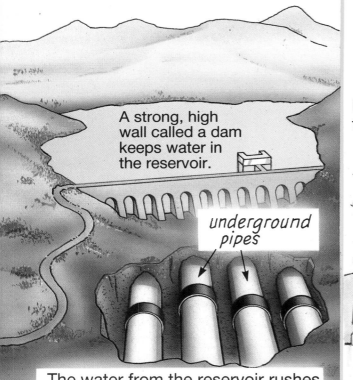

A strong, high wall called a dam keeps water in the reservoir.

underground pipes

When the turbine runner spins it works the generator and this makes the electricity.

The water from the reservoir rushes downhill, through huge pipelines. Some are about 33 feet wide.

Saving the water

top reservoir

Streams or rivers flow into the reservoir all the time and keep it full of water.	In hydro-electric power stations the water flows away, after it has been used to make electricity.

lower reservoir

Some power stations save the water and use it again and again.

The water works the turbines, then it runs into a lower reservoir.

The pump

Electricity works huge pumps. They push the water back up to the top reservoir, ready to be used again.

Fishing

The water which has been used in the power station is clean. Fish can live in the reservoir.

Going places

Electricity is used to work high speed trains, subway trains, ships and airplanes. It even works the control of space rockets.

Electric trains

Electric trains get electricity from overhead wires, or a third rail on the ground. It goes into motors which turn the wheels.

← overhead wires →

This Japanese "bullet" train can travel at 125 miles an hour.

Tracks and wires

Trollies pick up electric current from overhead wires.

Some trollies pick it up from an electric rail in a slot in the ground.

Subway trains are worked by electricity from extra rails.

On the sea and in the air

Electricity works special controls and instruments on ships and airplanes.

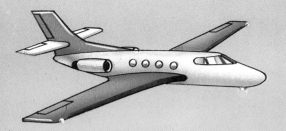

Electric circuits work dials and levers in an airplane.

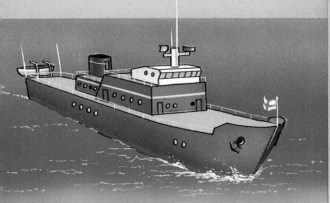

A ship needs electricity to give light and heat. It is also used to work the radio and control the steering.

Space travel

The Space Shuttle is fired into space by electric signals.

Electric circuits in a computer help the crew to fly the Shuttle and work scientific instruments.

65

Other electricity

There is a kind of electricity called static electricity. It does not flow through wires like electric current, but it does some amazing things.

Try this

Rub a plastic pen on a wool sweater for about 30 seconds.

Hold the pen very close to some small pieces of thin paper.

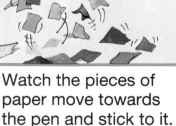

Watch the pieces of paper move towards the pen and stick to it.

Why it works

This works because static electricity builds up in the pen when you rub it against the wool.

It is the static electricity which pulls the paper towards the pen, making it jump, like magic.

Did you know?

Before a thunderstorm, static electricity builds up in storm clouds. When there is too much, it escapes as a flash of lightning.

Tall buildings have a metal strip down the outside, called a lightning conductor.

If lightning strikes a building which has a conductor, it travels through the metal, down to the ground.

Tiny sparks

Lightning hit a tree during a storm in South Dakota, America. Static electricity made the tree light up.

Tiny sparks twinkled on the end of each twig, like fairy lights.

Electricity in fish

An electric eel can make electricity in its body.

It stuns its prey with an electric shock, before eating it.

Power in the future

One day all the coal and oil which help make electrical power will be used up. Scientists are working to find new ways of making electricity.

Using the sun

Something called a solar panel can be put into your roof. It traps the sun's heat to warm the house.

Sunlight can make electricity using an invention called a solar cell.

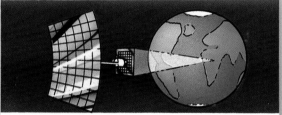

One day, scientists may put a solar collector, made of lots of solar cells, into space. The electricity made would be beamed to Earth.

Using the wind

The wind has powered windmills for hundreds of years. Now it is used to work special windmills which make electric power.

When the wind blows, it pushes against the huge blades and makes them turn. The moving blades work the generator to make electricity.

Using the waves

Scientists are working out how to get power from the movement of waves, far out at sea. It could make lots of electricity to use on land.

Some countries hope to build tidal power stations. These will make electricity using the flow of the tide, as it goes in and out.

High speed travel

In the future, electric trains may not need wheels. They will hover above special electric tracks.

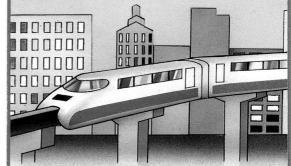

They will speed along at over 240 miles an hour.

Electric cars

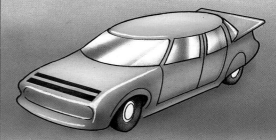

Scientists have built cars which run on electricity. But they need to work out many problems before all cars will run without gasoline.

Useful words

You can find these words in this part of the book. The pictures will help you remember what the words mean.

antenna

This picks up electrical signals from the air. If you have a television in your house, or a radio in your car, you need an antenna.

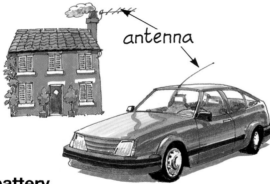

antenna

battery

This has special chemicals inside. They work together to make small amounts of electricity.

cables

These wires carry electric signals under the ground. They have a special covering to protect them.

circuit

An electric circuit is a path of wires. The electricity must travel all the way round to work something electrical.

filament

This is the very thin coil of wire inside a light bulb. When electricity flows through, it glows brightly.

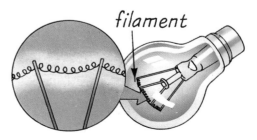

filament

generator

This machine makes electricity. Huge generators make electricity in power stations.

telephone exchange

This is where machines ring the telephone number you have dialled.

pylons

These are strong, steel towers which carry electric wires safely, high above the ground.

transformer

This changes the electricity to make it stronger or weaker.

reactor

This is the part of a nuclear power station where special fuel rods are used to make heat.

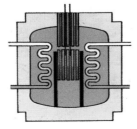

turbine

This is a kind of machine which is worked by water, steam or air, pushing against the blades.

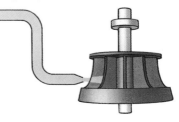

Picture puzzle

In this picture there are at least 14 things which need electricity to make them work. Can you find them?

There are two things which will not work when they are switched on. Can you see which two?

Answers

Room light, street light, car headlight, lamp, electric heater, television, radio, telephone, record player, digital watch, flashlight, vacuum cleaner, power drill, battery operated toy.

Things which will not work: The drill – it is not plugged in. The flashlight – the batteries are falling out.

72

WHAT'S UNDER THE GROUND?

Illustrated by Mike Pringle, Brin Edwards and John Scorey

CONTENTS

Susan Mayes

Under your feet

Under the ground there is a world you hardly ever see. Something is happening down there all the time.

People underground

People do different jobs under the ground. They dig and build, or mend things under the street. They even travel through specially made tunnels.

Animals

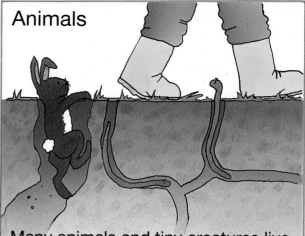

Many animals and tiny creatures live in the soil under your feet. Some of them come out to hunt or play. Others stay underground all the time.

Plants

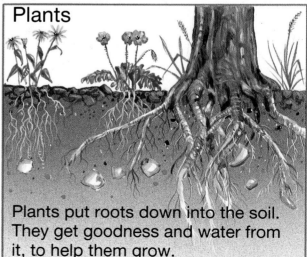

Plants put roots down into the soil. They get goodness and water from it, to help them grow.

Life long ago
The bones of huge creatures have been found under the ground. They were buried for millions of years.

Digging things up
Your home may be made from things which are dug out of the ground. So are lots of things you use every day.

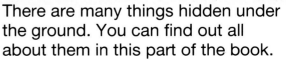

Dinosaur skeletons have been uncovered in some countries. They show us what lived long ago.

There are many things hidden under the ground. You can find out all about them in this part of the book.

Under the street

Pipes, tunnels and cables are put under the street to keep them out of the way. You cannot see them most of the time, but there are clues which tell you they are there.

A metal plate on a wall shows that there is a big underground water pipe nearby.

Rainwater runs through this grate. It goes down pipes which carry it away.

Under the metal cover is a room called a manhole. Pipes go through it, carrying fresh water.

Water pipes
Fresh water for you to drink and use is pumped through the mains pipe.

mains pipe

Another pipe joins the mains and takes the water into your home.

Drains and sewers
A drain is a pipe which carries dirty water and waste from your house.

Then the waste runs into bigger pipes. They are called sewers.

Storm drains
Rainwater flows through a grate and fills a pit under the street.

Garbage collects here.

The water runs into a pipe. This takes it to the storm drain.

Most telephone messages travel through underground cables.

When workers dig up the road you can often see electric cables or gas pipes under the ground.

Did you know?
Many telephone cables have thin glass threads inside. Your message goes along one of these.

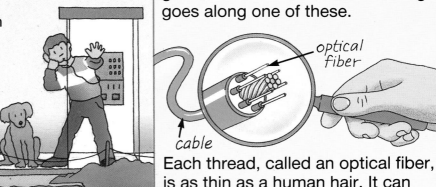

optical fiber

cable

Each thread, called an optical fiber, is as thin as a human hair. It can carry thousands of calls at one time.

Putting electricity underground
Electric cables carry power to homes, schools, factories, hospitals and shops. They often go underground.

First, deep trenches are dug in the street. Pipes called ducts are laid in them and covered with soil.

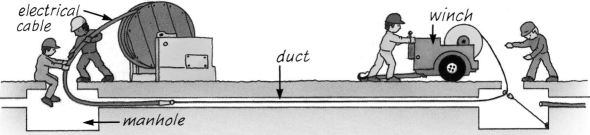

electrical cable

winch

duct

manhole

The electric cable is on a huge reel. One end is put down an electrical manhole and into the duct.

At the next manhole, a winch pulls the cable through. The end will be joined to a cable from another duct.

Tunnels for travel

Many cities in the world have subways. Thousands of people use them every day to get to places quickly and easily.

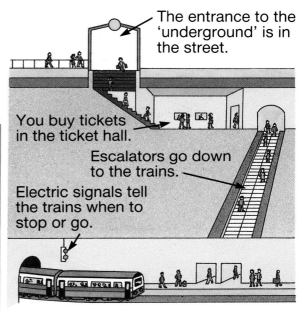

The entrance to the 'underground' is in the street.

You buy tickets in the ticket hall.

Escalators go down to the trains.

Electric signals tell the trains when to stop or go.

Building tunnels
The world's first subway was built in London, in 1863.

A huge trench was dug in the road. Subway lines were laid in it and covered with an arched roof. Then the road was built over the top again.

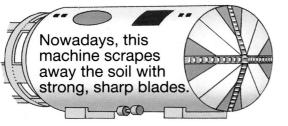

Nowadays, this machine scrapes away the soil with strong, sharp blades.

Today, tunnels are built much deeper under the ground. Machines can drill holes under buildings and rivers.

Did you know?
In some countries, road tunnels are built inside mountains. The longest one in the world is in Switzerland.

The St. Gotthard Road Tunnel goes through the Swiss Alps. It is just over 10 miles long.

The Channel Tunnel

The Channel Tunnel is really three tunnels. They go under the sea between Britain and France.

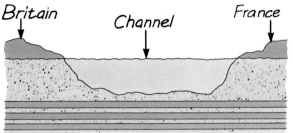

Britain   Channel   France

People in both countries dug the tunnels through the hard chalk. They finished work in 1994.

Trains carry passengers through two of the tunnels. They must not go faster than 100 miles an hour.

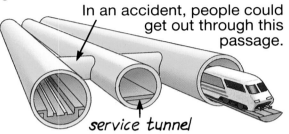

In an accident, people could get out through this passage.

service tunnel

The middle tunnel is called a service tunnel. Workers go through it when they make repairs.

Lining a tunnel

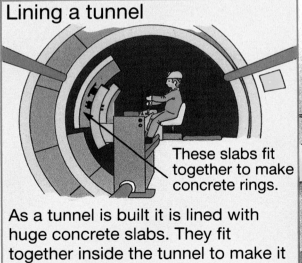

These slabs fit together to make concrete rings.

As a tunnel is built it is lined with huge concrete slabs. They fit together inside the tunnel to make it strong and to keep the damp out.

Electric cables are fixed to the tunnel walls. They work lights and machines.

Tractors and trucks drive around inside the tunnel.

Under your home

Some buildings have rooms underneath. A few homes are built underground. But nearly all buildings begin below the surface.

Building foundations

Builders make the foundations of a house first. These are built into the ground and the house is built on top. They stop the house from sinking.

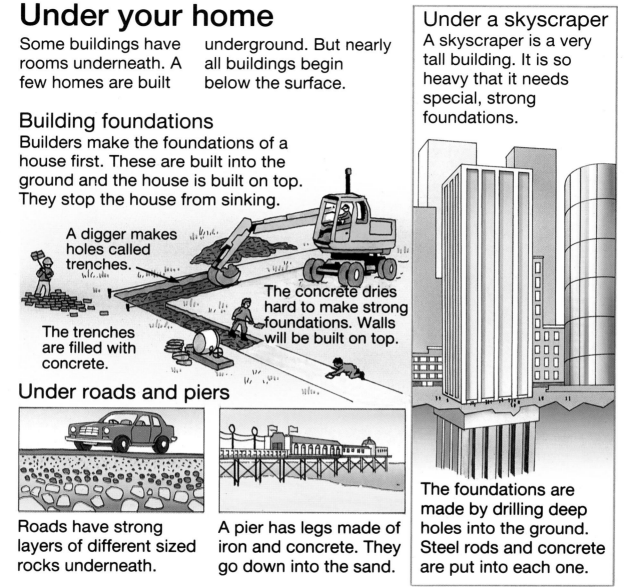

A digger makes holes called trenches.

The trenches are filled with concrete.

The concrete dries hard to make strong foundations. Walls will be built on top.

Under roads and piers

Roads have strong layers of different sized rocks underneath.

A pier has legs made of iron and concrete. They go down into the sand.

Under a skyscraper

A skyscraper is a very tall building. It is so heavy that it needs special, strong foundations.

The foundations are made by drilling deep holes into the ground. Steel rods and concrete are put into each one.

A city on water
Venice, in Italy, was built over a salty lake called a lagoon.

In Venice, people travel along canals.

Logs were pushed down into the muddy ground under the lagoon. Wood and stones were laid across the logs. The city was built on top.

Basements and cellars
Some buildings have rooms which are lower than the street. This underground part is the basement.

This is a wine cellar underneath a hotel.

A cellar is an underground room used for storing things. Wine is kept in a cellar as it is cool down there.

Underground homes
The Berber people live in Tunisia, Africa. They build underground homes.

The top rooms are used for storing things in.

The bottom rooms are for living in.

They find deep pits and burrow into the walls to make rooms. These stay cool in the hot daytime. On cold winter nights the rooms are warm.

Holes and burrows

Many animals tunnel down into the soil to make homes underground.

These homes are safe and hidden away. They have different names.

Badgers live in a home called a set. They rest there in the day and come out at night.

Lots of rabbits live together in a warren. It is made up of groups of burrows.

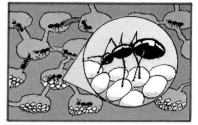

Ants live in an underground home called a nest. It is made of passages and rooms.

Made for digging
Burrowing animals have bodies which are very good at digging.

Rabbits use their front paws to burrow into the ground. They push the soil away with their back legs.

Moles have strong front legs. They can dig easily with their shovel-shaped feet.

Earthworms have strong muscles to pull them through the soil.

Moles live in the dark and are almost blind.

Living in hot places

Deserts are hot, dry places. Most small desert animals live in burrows in the daytime. They come out at night when the air is cooler.

The fennec fox hunts at night and rests in its burrow in the day.

The jerboa comes out to search for seeds and dry grass.

Keeping damp

An Australian desert frog sleeps in its burrow nearly all year.

A special covering of skin keeps it damp. It only comes out when it starts to rain.

Living in cold places

Animals live in some of the coldest places in the world. Many survive by eating a lot, then sleeping all winter. This is called hibernation.

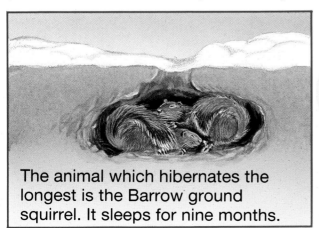

The animal which hibernates the longest is the Barrow ground squirrel. It sleeps for nine months.

Families of marmots hibernate inside their warm burrows. They make grass nests and block the way in.

What's in the soil?

Soil is really layers of stones, sand and clay. These come from rock which has been worn away by water and wind. This takes millions of years.

Nothing would grow without humus. This is made from dead plants and animals which have rotted away. The soil on top is full of humus.

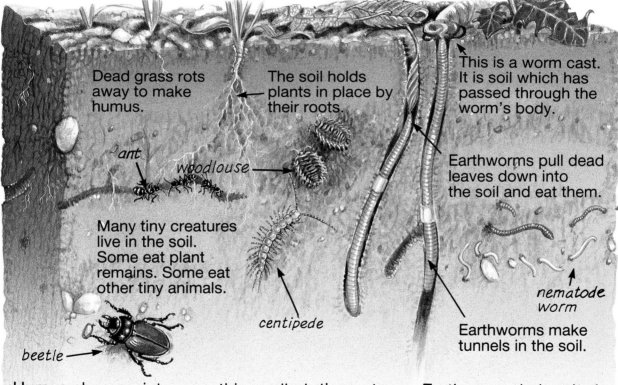

Dead grass rots away to make humus.

The soil holds plants in place by their roots.

This is a worm cast. It is soil which has passed through the worm's body.

ant

woodlouse

Earthworms pull dead leaves down into the soil and eat them.

Many tiny creatures live in the soil. Some eat plant remains. Some eat other tiny animals.

centipede

nematode worm

Earthworms make tunnels in the soil.

beetle

Humus changes into something called minerals. All living things need minerals to help them grow*. Minerals feed plants with goodness to make them strong. Earthworms help mix the minerals into the soil. Plants also need air and water. These get into the soil through tunnels made by worms.

*Calcium is a mineral, for example. It makes your teeth and bones strong.

Making a wormery

Fill a jar with layers of soil and sand. Make sure the soil is damp, then put some leaves on top.

Cover the jar with a cloth.

Put a few worms in the jar, then cover it up so it is dark. The worms will start to tunnel. In a few days the soil and sand will be mixed up.

Wet and dry soil

Sandy soil is dry because water drains through it. Desert plants grow well in this kind of soil.

cactus

sandy soil

They would not grow in soil with lots of clay in it. Clay soil holds water easily. It is wet and sticky.

Food under the ground

Gardeners often grow plants in the same place every year. The minerals which feed the plants get used up.

beetroot

potatoes

radishes

carrots

compost heap

Many gardeners put goodness back into the soil by digging in compost. This is made from plants which have been specially left to rot away.

Vegetables grow well in dark, rich soil. The ones in this picture are root vegetables. This means that the part you eat grows under the ground.

All about fossils

Fossils are the remains of animals and plants which lived millions of years ago. This picture shows an animal which died and sank to the sea bed. The soft parts of its body rotted away, but the bones were left.

sea

sand

sediment

bones

The bones were covered with sand and tiny grains called sediment. The sediment turned into hard rock and the bones were trapped inside.

Very slowly, minerals in the sediment changed the bones into fossils. These stayed buried for millions of years until the rocks were uncovered.

What fossils tell us

The fossils in these pictures helped scientists to guess what the first living things looked like.

trilobite fossil

stegosaurus fossil

The first animals lived in water. Trilobites were sea creatures with hard bodies made of segments.

Later, dinosaurs ruled the Earth. A stegosaurus had bony plates on its back. Some plates were 3 feet high.

Plants long ago

This plant fossil is over 50 million years old.

Some kinds of sediment could save plant shapes for ever. There are many fossil remains of the first plants.

Looking for fossils

Fossil hunters do not usually find anything as huge as a dinosaur. But they do find lots of other fossils.

This special hammer helps to get the fossil out.

Rocky beaches are good places to search. A rock may get worn away and part of a fossil is uncovered.

arsinoitherium fossil

fossil of a footprint

Millions of years later there were animals almost like those we see now. This one was like a rhinoceros.

The first kind of human lived around 2 million years ago. The oldest human fossils are from Africa.

Inside a cave

A cave is like an underground room. It is made by rainwater which wears rock away. Caves often form in limestone which wears away easily.

Water drips from the ceiling. It leaves minerals behind. Very slowly these begin to form rocky icicles called stalactites.

Drops with minerals in may hit the floor. They make rock towers called stalagmites.

An underground stream runs through this cave.

The water trickles down into holes and passages in the rock. It makes them bigger and bigger. A cave is a huge hole which has been made.

What lives in a cave?

Most animals living in the mouth of the cave also live in the outside world. Cave swallows fly in and out.

It is darker further inside. It is also damp and cool. Bats live here and come out to hunt at night.

Deep inside the cave it is dark all the time. Glow-worms may live in here. They make their own bright lights.

A hidden cave

The way into a cave is sometimes hidden. In 1940 two boys discovered a cave which nobody knew about.

The boys were walking their dog near Lascaux in France. They found the cave when the dog fell down the entrance which had bushes in front.

Cave paintings

The Lascaux cave has paintings on the ceiling and walls. Cave people did them thousands of years ago.

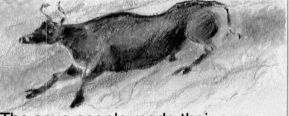

The cave people made their own paints and tools. They painted bulls, cows, deer, bison and horses. These were the animals they hunted.

Try this

Do a painting using tools and paints which you have made or found yourself. You will need:

You could also try painting using food coloring in a few drops of water.

Large scrap of paper or cardboard   water   soil in a pot   twigs

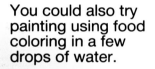

Mix a few drops of water into the soil. Cave people used colored earth to make paint. They mostly used red, yellow, brown, black and white.

Dip the twig brush into the paint and try painting on the cardboard with it. You may need to dip it in many times as you work, but keep going.

89

Useful things underground

People dig and drill for things far underground. Coal and oil help to make electricity, but they are also used to make lots of other things.

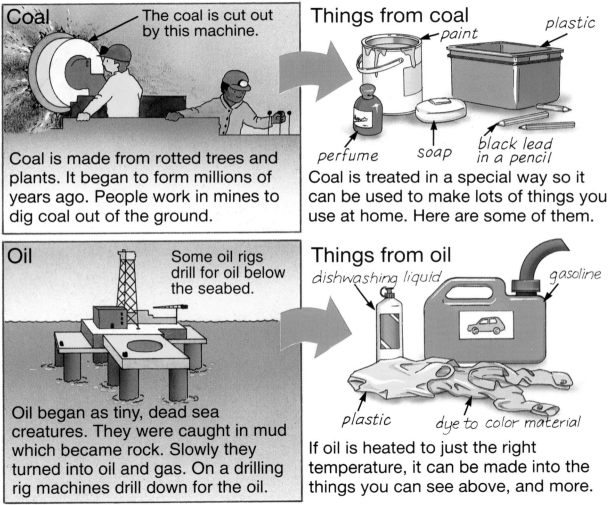

Coal

The coal is cut out by this machine.

Coal is made from rotted trees and plants. It began to form millions of years ago. People work in mines to dig coal out of the ground.

Things from coal

paint

plastic

perfume

soap

black lead in a pencil

Coal is treated in a special way so it can be used to make lots of things you use at home. Here are some of them.

Oil

Some oil rigs drill for oil below the seabed.

Oil began as tiny, dead sea creatures. They were caught in mud which became rock. Slowly they turned into oil and gas. On a drilling rig machines drill down for the oil.

Things from oil

dishwashing liquid

gasoline

plastic

dye to color material

If oil is heated to just the right temperature, it can be made into the things you can see above, and more.

Things for building

For thousands of years homes have been built using different kinds of rocks. They are dug out of the ground in places called quarries.

Clay is made from tiny grains of rock. Damp clay is made into shapes and baked hard to make tiles.

Glass is made by melting limestone, sand and something called soda.

Bricks are made from clay.

Building blocks are made of concrete.

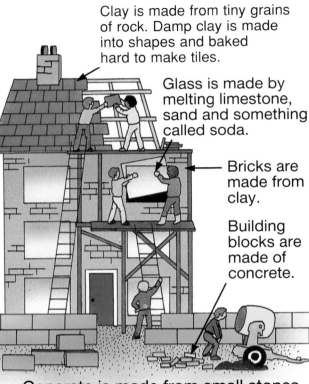

Concrete is made from small stones, sand and cement. These are mixed with water and left to harden. This makes a very strong building material.

Metal from the ground

Metal is found in rocks. You can find lots of metal things in your kitchen.

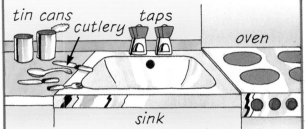

tin cans
cutlery
taps
oven
sink

Rock with metal in it is called ore. Some kinds of ore are heated in a special oven. The metal comes out as liquid ready for making things.

Did you know?

Jewels form deep inside the Earth where it is very hot. Minerals far underground turn into hard crystals.

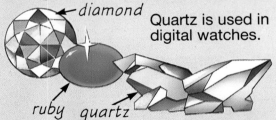

diamond

Quartz is used in digital watches.

ruby   quartz

These crystals are rough when they are taken out of the ground. They are cut and polished to make jewelry.

What's inside the Earth?

The Earth is like a ball with a hard, rocky crust. Some parts of the crust are weak and it often moves or cracks in these places.

Underneath the crust is the mantle. This is hot, soft rock which moves all the time.

crust
mantle
outer core   inner core

The middle of the Earth is called the core. The outside of the core is hot, runny metal. The inside is hard metal. This is the hottest part.

Sometimes the inside of the Earth moves so much that amazing things happen on the surface, where we live.

Volcanoes

A volcano is made when hot, runny rock is pushed up from inside the Earth. It hardens into a cone shape.

This volcano is erupting. Hot rock called lava is bursting out of it.

This lava will cool and harden into a layer of rock. The volcano gets bigger each time it erupts.

crater

Some cone-shaped mountains are old volcanoes. They are extinct. This means they do not erupt any more.

Shaking ground

An earthquake is when the ground shakes very hard. It happens when the Earth's crust moves suddenly.

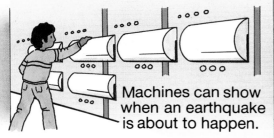

Machines can show when an earthquake is about to happen.

In countries with many earthquakes the buildings must be specially made, so they do not fall down.

Hot water

In some places a fountain of hot water shoots out of the ground. It is called a geyser. The water is heated by hot rocks in the Earth's crust.

This geyser in America spouts water about once an hour.

In some countries they use underground heat to make electricity.

Buried treasure

Vesuvius is a volcano in Naples, Italy. It first erupted nearly two thousand years ago, in Roman times.

These are Roman treasures.

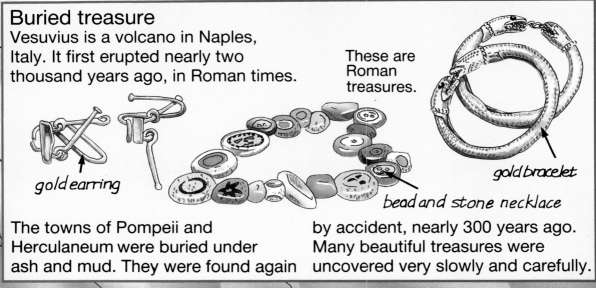

gold earring

gold bracelet

bead and stone necklace

The towns of Pompeii and Herculaneum were buried under ash and mud. They were found again by accident, nearly 300 years ago. Many beautiful treasures were uncovered very slowly and carefully.

Underground facts

On this page you can find out about some amazing things underground.

The longest tunnel

The longest tunnel is almost 169km (105 miles) long. It carries water to New York City, USA.

It is just over 4m (13ft) high. That is about as high as two people.

The first bird

A fossil of the first bird that ever lived was dug up in Germany, in 1861. The bird was called Archaeopteryx. It lived over 150 million years ago. You can even see the feathers on the wings and body.

Going down

A man went almost 4km (2½ miles) into the ground in a mine in South Africa. This is the deepest that anyone has ever been.

The biggest cave

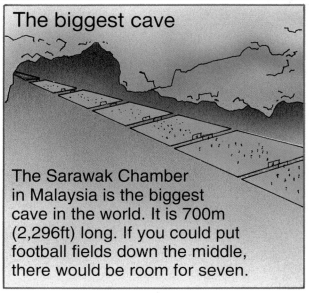

The Sarawak Chamber in Malaysia is the biggest cave in the world. It is 700m (2,296ft) long. If you could put football fields down the middle, there would be room for seven.